This book is dedicated to all the kids at Rockford Iqra school and any Islamic institution that has people who want to learn the beautiful meaning of the Quran.

وقل ربي زدني علما

And say, "Oh my lord, increase my knowledge"
When I hit 40 I realized I needed to do something more for my hereafter. The Quran is easy to forget if you don't keep practicing it, but the meaning of it and the message that Allah sent can be remembered and embodied in our lives. That's why I decided to write this book to focus on the lessons that we can learn from the surahs.
I believe that you will reap what you sow in kids. From my experience, I know that we should never underestimate little kids-they are bright and absorb whatever information you give them. The Quran is the most important resource for all Muslims, young and old. It is our guidance until the day of judgment, and we can not truly benefit from it until we understand it. Instead of reading it like any other book, we should read it in order to understand it and apply it to our lives. I tried to make this book as kid-friendly as possible by adding pictures to help the kids understand and enjoy it. In sha Allah you can benefit from this book in some way and pass on what you have learned to others.

NOW I CAN
UNDERSTAND
THE QURAN

Compiled by Hana Abaz

Surah Al-Humazah: The Backbiters

بِسْمِ ٱللَّهِ ٱلرَّحْمَـٰنِ ٱلرَّحِيمِ

وَيْلٌ لِّكُلِّ **هُمَزَةٍ** لُّمَزَةٍ

Waylul-likulli **humaza** tillumazah

هُمَزَةٍ

It will be very bad for the one who
backbites or mocks others

ٱلَّذِى جَمَعَ **مَالًا** وَعَدَّدَهُۥ

Allathee jama'a **maala**
wa 'addadah

مَالًا

Who collects money in a
greedy way and counts it
over and over

يَحْسَبُ أَنَّ مَالَهُ أَخْلَدَهُ

Yahsabu anna
maalahooo **akhladah**

أَخْلَدَ

They think that their money will
make them live forever

كَلَّا لَيُنْبَذَنَّ فِى ٱلْحُطَمَةِ

Kallaa; **layumbathanna**
fil hutamah

لَيُنْبَذَنَّ

Definitely not! A person like
that will be thrown into the
Crusher

وَمَآ أَدْرَىٰكَ مَا الْحُطَمَةُ

Wa maa adraaka mal-**hutamah**

الْحُطَمَةُ

And do you not know what the
Crusher is?

نَارُ ٱللَّهِ ٱلْمُوقَدَةُ

Naarul laahil-mooqada

نَارُ

It is Allah's burning fire

ٱلَّتِى تَطَّلِعُ عَلَى ٱلْأَفْئِدَةِ

Allatee tattali'u 'ala **alaf'idah**

ٱلْأَفْئِدَةِ

Which reaches into the hearts

8

إِنَّهَا عَلَيْهِم مُّؤْصَدَةٌ

Innahaa 'alaihim
mu'sada

مُّؤْصَدَةٌ

It will be shut on them

9

فِى عَمَدٍ مُّمَدَّدَةٍ

Fee **'amad**im
mumaddadah

عَمَدٍ

Closed tightly with long bars

Match the word with the picture

مُّؤْصَدَةٌ

ٱلْهُمَزَة

مَالَ

ٱلْأُفْئِدَةِ

Color each picture and rewrite the word

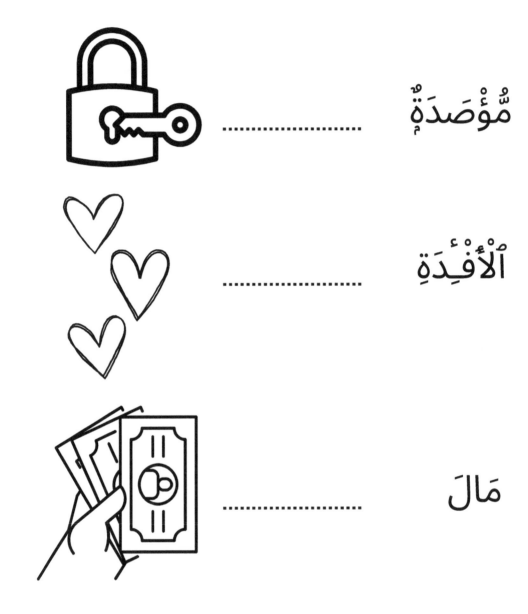

مُّؤْصَدَةٌ

....

ٱلْأَفْئِدَةِ

....

مَالَ

....

Surah Al-'Asr:
The Passing Time

بِسْمِ ٱللَّهِ ٱلرَّحْمَـٰنِ ٱلرَّحِيمِ

وَٱلْعَصْرِ

Wal 'asr

ٱلْعَصْرِ

(Allah swears) by the
passing time

إِنَّ ٱلْإِنسَـٰنَ لَفِى خُسْرٍ

Innal insaana lafee **khusr**

خُسْرٍ

For sure, humans will
be in complete loss

15

إِلَّا ٱلَّذِينَ ءَامَنُواْ وَعَمِلُواْ ٱلصَّلِحَتِ

Illal latheena aamanoo
wa'amilus saalihaati

عَمِلُواْ ٱلصَّلِحَتِ

Except those who have
belief and do good deeds

16

وَتَوَاصَوْاْ بِٱلْحَقِّ
وَتَوَاصَوْاْ بِٱلصَّبْرِ

wa tawaasaw **bilhaqqi**
wa tawaasaw **bissabr**

ٱلْحَقِّ

ٱلصَّبْرِ

And encourage each other to tell the truth and encourage each other to be patient

17

Number the pictures in the order that they are mentioned in the surah

Color the pictures that show good deeds

Surah At- Takathur: Competition for More

بِسْمِ ٱللَّهِ ٱلرَّحْمَـٰنِ ٱلرَّحِيمِ

أَلْهَىٰكُمُ ٱلتَّكَاثُرُ

Al haakumut **takathur**

ٱلتَّكَاثُرُ

Always competing for more distracts
you from Allah SWT

حَتَّىٰ زُرْتُمُ ٱلْمَقَابِرَ

Hatta zurtumu **al-maqaabir**

ٱلْمَقَابِرَ

Until you visit the graves

22

كَلَّا سَوْفَ تَعْلَمُونَ

Kalla sawfa ta'lamoon

ثُمَّ كَلَّا سَوْفَ تَعْلَمُونَ

Thumma kalla sawfa ta'lamoon

ثُمَّ

But no, you will soon know.
Again no, you will soon know

كَلَّا لَوْ تَعْلَمُونَ عِلْمَ ٱلْيَقِينِ

Kalla law ta'lamoona 'ilma
alyaqeen

ٱلْيَقِينِ

If you knew for sure (that your
actions matter, you would have
done better)

لَتَرَوُنَّ ٱلْجَحِيمَ

Latara-wun nal
jaheem

ٱلْجَحِيمَ

That you would see the Hellfire

ثُمَّ لَتَرَوُنَّهَا عَيْنَ ٱلْيَقِينِ

Thumma latara wunnaha
'ayn alyaqeen

And then later, you will see it
with your own eyes

ثُمَّ لَتُسْـَٔلُنَّ يَوْمَئِذٍ عَنِ ٱلنَّعِيمِ

Thumma **latusalunna** yawma-ithin 'anin na'eem

تُسْـَٔلُنَّ

Then, on that day, you will be asked about your blessings

Color each picture and rewrite the word

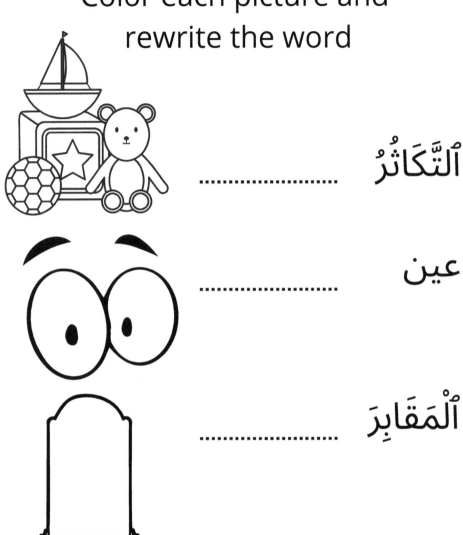

ٱلتَّكَاثُرُ ....

عين ....

ٱلْمَقَابِرَ ....

ٱلْيَقِينِ ....

Write or draw three things people like to compete in during this life:

When do people realize that their competition is not beneficial?

Surah Al-Qari'ah: The Loud Disaster

بِسْمِ ٱللَّهِ ٱلرَّحْمَـٰنِ ٱلرَّحِيمِ

ٱلْقَارِعَةُ

Al qaari'ah

مَا ٱلْقَارِعَةُ

Mal qaariah

The Loud Disaster.
What is the Loud Disaster?

وَمَآ أَدْرَىٰكَ مَا ٱلْقَارِعَةُ

Wa **maa adraaka** mal qaari'ah

What can make you know?

مَآ أَدْرَىٰكَ

And how will you know what the Loud Disaster is?

يَوْمَ يَكُونُ ٱلنَّاسُ كَٱلْفَرَاشِ ٱلْمَبْثُوثِ

Yawma ya koonun naasu
kalfarashil mabthooth

فَرَاشِ

On that day, the people will be
like moths everywhere

وَتَكُونُ **ٱلجِبَالُ** كَٱلْعِهْنِ ٱلْمَنفُوشِ

Wa ta koonul **jibalu** kal ‘ihnil manfoosh

ٱلْجِبَالُ

And the mountains will be like fluffy wool

فَأَمَّا مَن ثَقُلَتْ مَوَٰزِينُهُ

Fa-amma man thaqulat
mawazeenuh

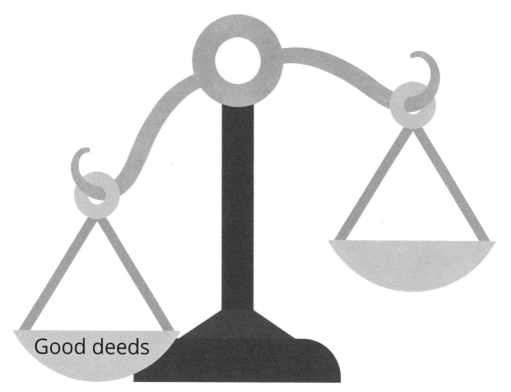

Good deeds

مَوَٰزِينُ

So whoever's scale is heavy with
good deeds

فَهُوَ فِى عِيشَةٍ رَّاضِيَةٍ

Fahuwa fee 'ishatir **raadiyah**

رَّاضِيَ

They will live a life
full of enjoyment

وَأَمَّا مَنْ خَفَّتْ مَوَازِينُهُ

Wa amma man **khaffat** mawa zeenuh

خَفَّ

But those whose scale is
light with good deeds

فَأُمُّهُ هَاوِيَةٌ

Fa-ummuhu haawiyah

هَاوِيَةٌ

He will be in the
bottom of the Hellfire

وَمَآ أَدْرَىٰكَ مَا هِيَهْ

Wa **maa adraaka**

maa hiyah

مَآ أَدْرَىٰكَ

And do you know what it is?

نَارٌ حَامِيَةٌ

Naarun hamiyah

نَارٌ

It is the burning fire

Match each word with
the correct picture

هَاوِيَةٌ

نَارٌ

مَوْزِينٌ

Color each picture and rewrite the word

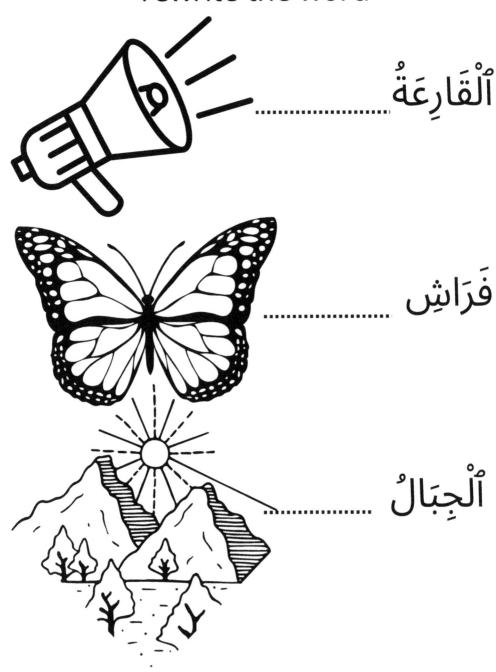

ٱلْقَارِعَةُ ....

فَرَاشٍ ....

ٱلْجِبَالُ ....

Write 3 good deeds on one hand of the scale and 3 bad deeds on the other

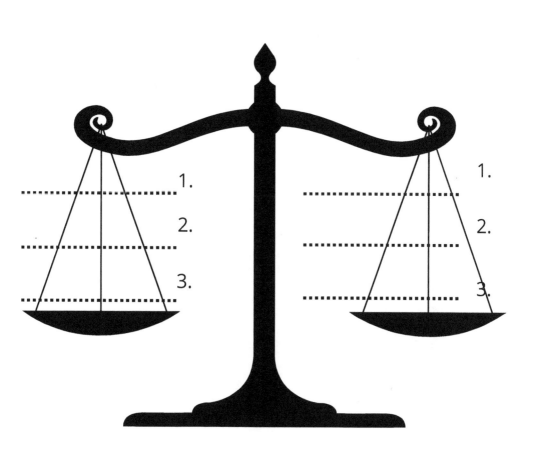

1.

2.

3.

1.

2.

3.

Surah Al-Adiyat: The Running Horses

بِسْمِ ٱللَّهِ ٱلرَّحْمَـٰنِ ٱلرَّحِيمِ

وَٱلْعَـٰدِيَـٰتِ ضَبْحًا

Wal'aadiyaati dabha

ٱلْعَـٰدِيَـٰتِ

(Allah swears) by the running
horses that breathe heavily

46

فَٱلْمُورِيَٰتِ قَدْحًا

Fal moori yaati **qadha**

قَدْحًا

Sparks of fire will come from their hooves

فَٱلْمُغِيرَٰتِ صُبْحًا

Fal mugheeraati **subha**

صُبْحًا

Fighting their enemies from the early morning

فَأَثَرْنَ بِهِ نَقْعًا

Fa atharna bihee **naq'a**

نَقْعًا

They made dust fly everywhere
from their running

49

فَوَسَطْنَ بِهِ جَمْعًا

Fawa satna bihee **jam'a**

جَمْعًا

They put themselves in the middle
of their enemies (because they
were brave)

إِنَّ ٱلْإِنسَـٰنَ لِرَبِّهِۦ لَكَنُودٌ

Innal-insana lirabbihee la**kanood**

كَنُودٌ

For sure, humans are ungrateful to their Lord

وَإِنَّهُۥ عَلَىٰ ذَٰلِكَ لَشَهِيدٌ

Wa innahu 'alaa thaalika
la shaheed

شَهِيدٌ

And the human is a witness
to that (he knows it)

وَإِنَّهُۥ لِحُبِّ ٱلْخَيْرِ لَشَدِيدٌ

Wa innahu **lihubbi**l khayri la shadeed

حُبِّ

And he loves money too much

أَفَلَا يَعْلَمُ إِذَا بُعْثِرَ مَا فِى ٱلْقُبُورِ

Afala ya'lamu itha b'uthira ma fil**quboor**

ٱلْقُبُورِ

Do they not know that when everything from their grave will come out

وَحُصِّلَ مَا فِى ٱلصُّدُورِ

Wa hussila maa fis **sudoor**

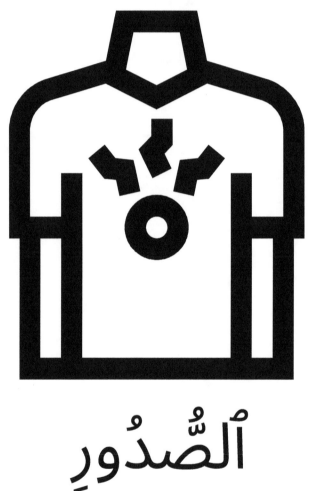

ٱلصُّدُورِ

And whatever they hide in their
heart will come out

55

إِنَّ رَبَّهُمْ بِهِمْ يَوْمَئِذٍ لَّخَبِيرٌ

Inna rabbahum bihim
yawma 'itnin **lakhabeer**

خَبِيرٌ

For sure, their lord will know
everything about them on that day

Match the word
with the correct picture

صُبْحًا

ٱلْعَدِيَتِ

ٱلْقُبُورِ

Color each picture and rewrite the word

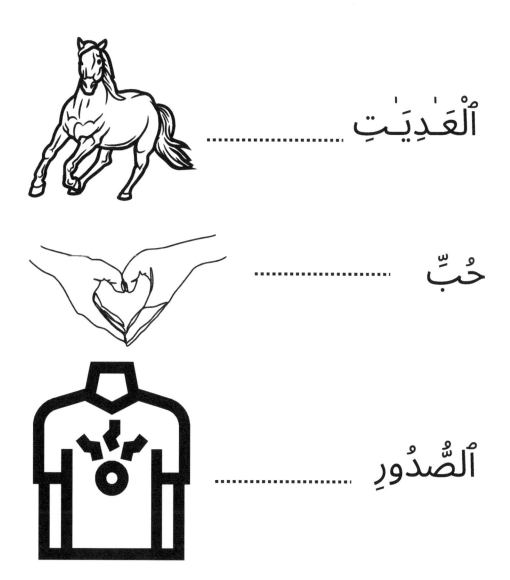

ٱلْعَدِيَتِ ....

حُبٌّ ....

ٱلصُّدُورِ ....

Surah Az-zalzalah: The Earthquake

بِسْمِ ٱللَّهِ ٱلرَّحْمَـٰنِ ٱلرَّحِيمِ

إِذَا زُلْزِلَتِ ٱلْأَرْضُ زِلْزَالَهَا

ithaa zul zilatil **ardu** zil zaalaha

ٱلْأَرْضُ

When the Earth is shaken really
badly by the final earthquake

وَأَخْرَجَتِ ٱلْأَرْضُ أَثْقَالَهَا

Wa akh rajatil ardu **athqaalaha**

أَثْقَالَهَا

And when the Earth throws out
everything heavy inside it

وَقَالَ **الْإِنْسَانُ** مَا لَهَا

Wa qaalal **insaanu** ma laha

الْإِنْسَانُ

And the humans ask "What is wrong with it?"

يَوْمَئِذٍ تُحَدِّثُ أَخْبَارَهَا

Yawmaa ithin tuhaddithu **akhbaar**aha

أَخْبَارَ

On that day, the Earth will tell its news

بِأَنَّ رَبَّكَ أَوْحَىٰ لَهَا

Bi-anna **rabbaka** awhaa laha

رَبَّ

Only because your Lord told it
to do that

يَوْمَئِذٍ يَصْدُرُ النَّاسُ أَشْتَاتًا لِيُرَوْا أَعْمَالَهُمْ

Yawma ithiny yas durun naasu **ashtata**l liyuraw a'maalahum

أَشْتَاتًا

On that day, people will come forward in different groups to see the results of their actions

فَمَنْ يَعْمَلْ مِثْقَالَ ذَرَّةٍ خَيْرًا يَرَهُ

Famay ya'mal mithqala tharratin **khayr**ay-yarah

خَيْر

And whoever does any small good deed will see it

وَمَنْ يَعْمَلْ مِثْقَالَ ذَرَّةٍ شَرًّا يَرَهُ

Wa maiy-y'amal mithqala tharratin **sharr**ay-yarah

شَرّ

And whoever does any small bad deed will see it

Match the picture with the correct word

ٱلْأَرْضُ

الزَلْزَلَة

الإنْسان

Color each picture and rewrite the word

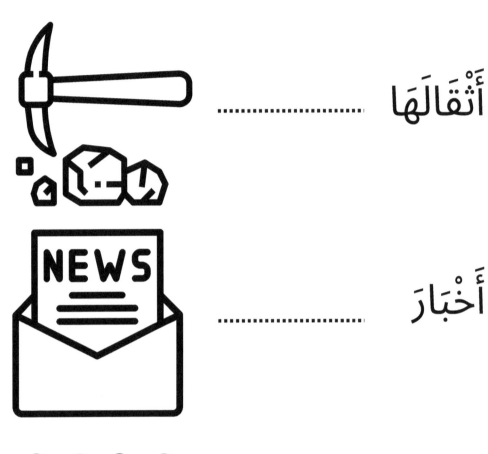

أَثْقَالَهَا ....

أَخْبَارَ ....

أَشْتَاتًا ....

Cross out the bad deed(s)

Cross out the bad deed(s)

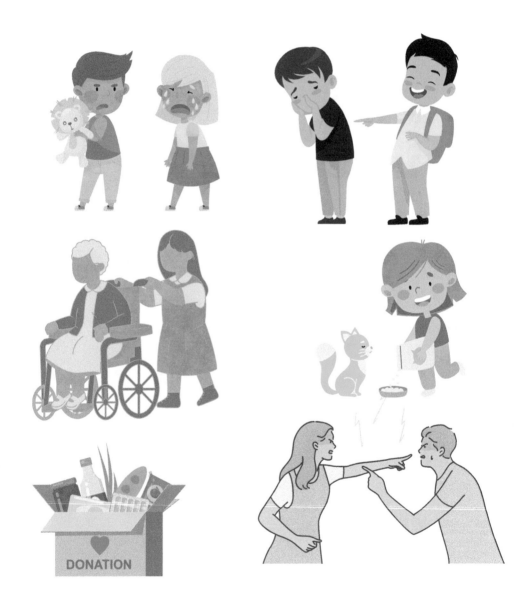

Surah Al-Qadr:
The Night of Power

بِسْمِ ٱللَّهِ ٱلرَّحْمَـٰنِ ٱلرَّحِيمِ

إِنَّآ أَنزَلْنَـٰهُ فِى **لَيْلَةِ** ٱلْقَدْرِ

Innaa anzalnaahu fee **laylati** lqadr

لَيْلَةِ

We sent down the Quran during the Night of Power

وَمَآ أَدْرَىٰكَ مَا لَيْلَةُ ٱلْقَدْرِ

Wa maa adraaka ma lailatu **alqadr**

القدر

And do you know what the
Night of Power is?

لَيْلَةُ ٱلْقَدْرِ خَيْرٌ مِّنْ أَلْفِ شَهْرٍ

Laylatul qadri khayrum
min alfee **shahr**

شَهْر

The Night of Power is better than a
thousand months

تَنَزَّلُ **ٱلْمَلَـٰٓئِكَةُ** وَٱلرُّوحُ فِيهَا بِإِذْنِ رَبِّهِم مِّن كُلِّ أَمْرٍ

Tanazzal **ulmalaa-ikatu** war roohu feeha bi izni-rab bihim min kulli amr

ٱلْمَلَـٰٓئِكَةُ

The angels and Holy Spirit (angel Jibreel) will come down with the permission of Allah with every matter

سَلَـٰمٌ هِيَ حَتَّىٰ مَطْلَعِ ٱلْفَجْرِ

Salaamun hiya hattaa
mat la'il fajr

سلام

There is peace
until dawn comes

Color each picture and rewrite each word

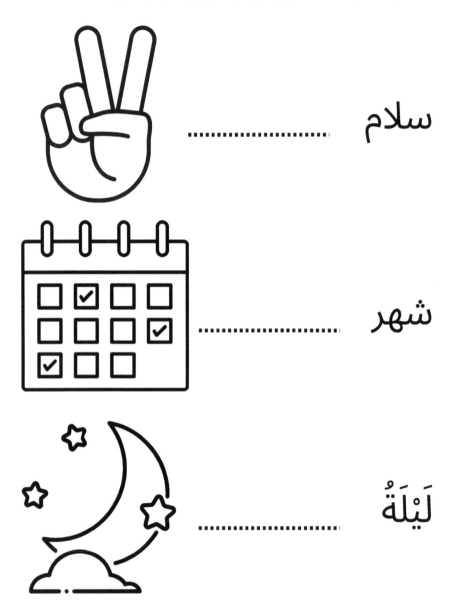

سلام ....

شهر ....

لَيْلَةُ ....

Match each picture with the correct word

لَيْلَةُ

شهر

ٱلْمَلَـٰئِكَةُ

Surah Al Alaq: The Tiny Thing in a Mom's Stomach

بِسْمِ ٱللَّهِ ٱلرَّحْمَـٰنِ ٱلرَّحِيمِ

ٱقْرَأْ بِٱسْمِ رَبِّكَ ٱلَّذِى خَلَقَ

Iqra bismi rab bikal lathee khalaq

ٱقْرَأْ

Read, in the name of your Lord
who created [you]

خَلَقَ ٱلْإِنسَـٰنَ مِنْ عَلَقٍ

Khalaqal insaana min 'alaq

عَلَقٍ

He created humans from a tiny
thing in their mom's stomach

أَقْرَأْ وَرَبُّكَ ٱلْأَكْرَمُ

Iqra wa rab buka **alakram**

ٱلْأَكْرَمُ

Read, and your lord is the most generous

ٱلَّذِى عَلَّمَ بِٱلْقَلَمِ

Al lathee 'allama bil
qalam

ٱلْقَلَمِ

The one who taught
by the pen

عَلَّمَ ٱلْإِنسَٰنَ مَا لَمْ يَعْلَمْ

'Al lama alinsaana ma lam y'alam

عَلَّمَ

He taught humans what they don't know

كَلَّآ إِنَّ ٱلْإِنسَـٰنَ لَيَطْغَىٰٓ

Kallaa innal insaana **layatghaa**

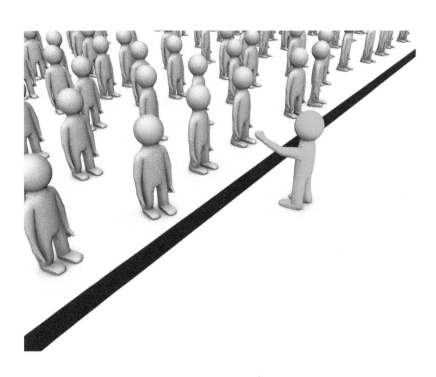

يَطْغَىٰٓ

Definitely, humans will cross the lines

أَن رَّعَاهُ ٱسْتَغْنَىٰٓ

Ar-ra aahu **staghnaa**

ٱسْتَغْنَىٰٓ

When he thinks he doesn't need anyone's help

إِنَّ إِلَىٰ رَبِّكَ ٱلرُّجْعَىٰٓ

Innna ilaa rabbik **arruj'aa**

ٱلرُّجْعَىٰٓ

To your Lord is the return

أَرَءَيْتَ ٱلَّذِى يَنْهَى

Ara-aytal lathee **yanhaa**

يَنْهَى

Have you seen the one who
prevents

عَبْدًا إِذَا صَلَّىٰٓ

'Abdan itha **sallaa**

صَلَّىٰٓ

A servant from praying

أَرَءَيْتَ إِن كَانَ عَلَى **ٱلْهُدَىٰٓ**

Ara-ayta in kana 'ala **alhudaa**

أَوْ أَمَرَ بِٱلتَّقْوَىٰٓ

Au amara bit taqwaa

ٱلْهُدَىٰٓ

Have you seen if he is on the path
of guidance? Or if he tells people to
do good?

أَرَءَيْتَ إِن كَذَّبَ وَتَوَلَّىٓ

Ara-ayta in **kathaba** wa ta walla

كَذَّبَ

Have you seen if he denies or turns away?

أَلَمْ يَعْلَم بِأَنَّ ٱللَّهَ يَرَىٰ

Alam y'alam bi-an nal lahaa **yaraa**

يَرَىٰ

Doesn't he know that Allah sees everything?

كَلَّا لَئِن لَّمْ يَنتَهِ لَنَسْفَعًا بِالنَّاصِيَةِ

Kalla la illam yantahi la nasfa'am bin **nasiyah**

نَاصِيَةٍ

If he does not stop, we will drag him by the hairs of his forehead

نَاصِيَةٍ كَـٰذِبَةٍ خَاطِئَةٍ

Nasiyatin kathi batin **khaatiah**

خَاطِئَةٍ

A lying and sinful forehead

فَلْيَدْعُ نَادِيَهُ

Fal yad'u naadiyah

HELP

فَلْيَدْعُ

So let him call his group

سَنَدْعُ ٱلزَّبَانِيَةَ

Sanad 'uz **zabaaniyah**

ٱلزَّبَانِيَةَ

We will call the guardians of Hellfire

كَلَّا لَا تُطِعْهُ **وَٱسْجُدْ** وَٱقْتَرِب

Kalla; la tuti'hu **wasjud** waqtarib

وَٱسْجُدْ

Again no, never obey him and instead keep making sujud and getting closer to Allah

Color each picture and rewrite the word

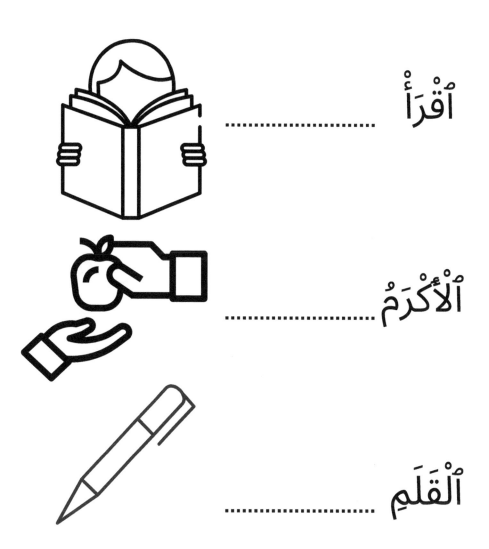

اَقْرَأْ

....

اَلْأَكْرَمُ

....

اَلْقَلَمِ

....

Color each picture and rewrite the word

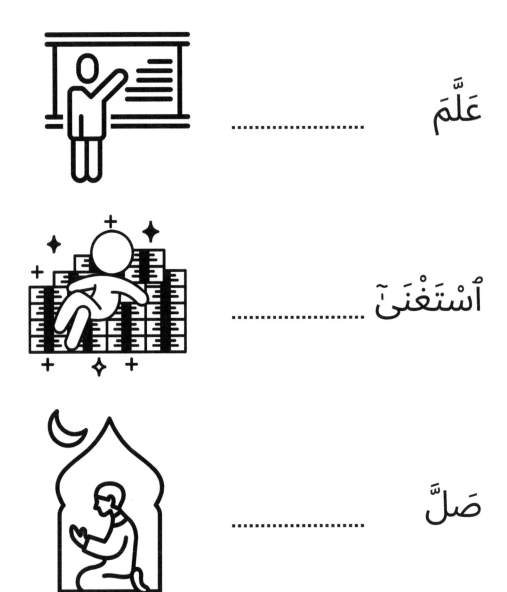

عَلَّمَ   ....

اِسْتَغْنَىٓ   ....

صَلَّ   ....

How many times is the word "ara'aeta repeated in surah Al-Alaq?

What is the name of the guardian of the Hellfire?

Write down three examples of things people do that are considered crossing the line

1.

2.

3.

Surah At-teen: The Fig

بِسْمِ ٱللَّهِ ٱلرَّحْمَـٰنِ ٱلرَّحِيم

وَٱلتِّينِ وَٱلزَّيْتُونِ

Wat teeni waz **zaytoon**

ٱلزَّيْتُونِ

(Allah swears) by the figs
and the olives

وَطُورِ سِينِينَ

Wa **toor**i sineen

طُورِ

And by the mountain of Sinai

وَهَـٰذَا ٱلْبَلَدِ ٱلْأُمِينِ

Wa haathal **balad-il ameen**

ٱلْبَلَدِ ٱلْأُمِينِ

And by the secure city of Mecca

لَقَدْ خَلَقْنَا ٱلْإِنسَـٰنَ فِىٓ أَحْسَنِ تَقْوِيمٍ

Laqad khalaqnal **insaan**a fee ahsani taqweem

الْإِنْسَانُ

For sure, we have created humans in the best form

ثُمَّ رَدَدْنٰهُ أَسْفَلَ سَفِلِينَ

Thumma ra dad naahu **asfala** saafileen

أَسْفَلَ

Then we will return him to the lowest of the low (in Hell)

إلَّا ٱلَّذِينَ **عَامَنُوا** وَعَمِلُوا ٱلصَّـٰلِحَـٰتِ فَلَهُمْ أَجْرٌ غَيْرُ مَمْنُونٍ

Ill-lal latheena **aamanoo** wa 'amilus saalihaati; falahum ajrun ghairu mamnoon

عَامَنُوا

Except those who have belief and do good deeds; they will have endless rewards

فَمَا يُكَذِّبُكَ بَعْدُ بِٱلدِّينِ

Fama yu kathibuka b'adu bid deen

أَلَيْسَ ٱللَّهُ بِأَحْكَمِ **ٱلْحَـٰكِمِينَ**

Alay sal laahu bi-ahkam **alhaakimeen**

حَـٰكِم

What makes you deny the Day of
Judgment?
Isn't Allah the most fair judge?

Color each picture and rewrite the word

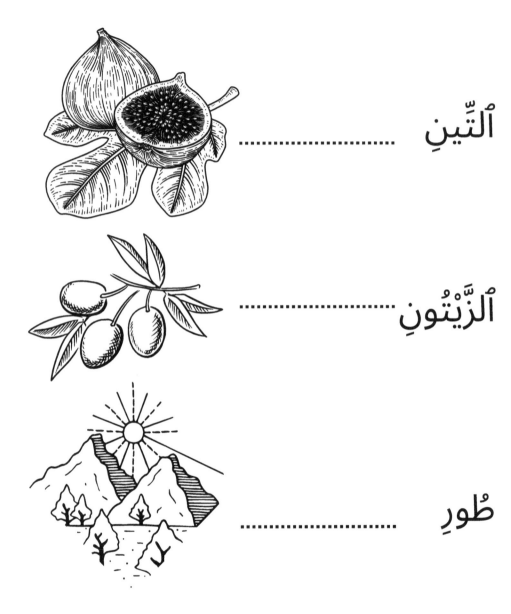

ٱلتِّينِ ....

ٱلزَّيْتُونِ ....

طُورِ ....

Match each word with the correct picture

ٱلزَّيْتُونِ

الْإِنْسَانُ

ٱلْبَلَدِ ٱلْأُمِينِ

What is the name of the Prophet that Allah SWT talked to on the Mountain of Sinai?

What is the secure city?

Sources:

1) Khattab, M. (2019). The clear quran for kids. Furqaan Institute of Quranic Education.

2) Quran transliteration: Making it easy to read Quran. My Islam. (2022, May 2). Retrieved August 25, 2022, from https://myislam.org/quran-transliteration/

3) 'Umar Ibn Kathīr Ismā'īl ibn, Mubārakfūrī Ṣafī al-Raḥmān, & 'Umar Ibn Kathīr Ismā'īl ibn. (2000). Tafsir ibn Kathir: (abridged). Darussalam.

Acknowledgements

First and foremost I would like to thank Allah SWT for making this journey possible. As the Prophet SAW said, من لا يشكر الناس لا يشكر الله: whoever does not thank the people does not thank Allah. I can't thank Allah enough for all the support, love, and help that I got from my friends and family. Without them, I couldn't have compiled this book.

Special thanks to my sweet youngest daughter, Ruydah, my cat-lover, for helping me put this book together. Thank you to my princess and business girl, my middle daughter, Amirah, who introduced me to Canva and took care of the production and printing process. Thank you to my wise eldest daughter Raneem for helping me with the English translation. Thanks to my middle son Hamza for helping with surah Al'adeat. Thank you to my husband, Dr. Zaher Qassem, who believed in me and was patient and supporting. Thank you to my BFF Ibtisam Altayeh for always standing with me, especially during the hardest times in my life. Thank you to the principals of Rockford Iqra school-Mona Nizamuddin and Ronald Hassan-for their support and encouragement. And thanks to my friends who believed in me and for those who didn't, because it just made me stronger.

May Allah reward everyone who helped me finish this book and may Allah allow everyone to benefit from my work. May Allah make it a Sadaqa Jareea for me, my parents, my husband, my kids, my brothers, and all the Muslims around the world. Ameen.

About the compiler:
Hana Abazid is a Syrian American Muslim who is married and has 6 amazing kids. She studied Islamic law at Damascus University. She has a masters degree in teaching English as a Second Language from Marshall University in West Virginia. She also has a Quran Tahfeez Certification with Tajweed. She is passionate about teaching Quran and Islamic manners to kids. She LOVES kids and LOVES working with kids.

She created a YouTube channel with her Iqra students called "Iqra Squad." Feel free to check out the channel and take a look at what she is teaching her students.

A word from the compiler:
"Every subject has its own textbook and I was surprised to see that Quran did not have its own separate curriculum, even though the Quran is the most important book. I remembered the saying 'if you need a change BE the change' so I decided to do it myself. With my limited technology skills but with a BIG heart and help from my amazing kids, I was able to create this book Alhamdulillah. I wanted to make something that would be attractive to first graders and kids in general, so I made it full of colors and pictures. In shaa Allah my goal is to create a Quran curriculum up to 8th grade, adjusting the curriculum for each age group such as by adding some tajweed rules and lessons learned from the Surah for older students. May Allah accept all our good deeds. And lastly, whatever good you find in this book is from Allah and whatever bad is from myself and shaytan."

CPSIA information can be obtained
at www.ICGtesting.com
Printed in the USA
LVHW071929051122
732457LV00032B/630